# Who?

Lewis Holifield

BookLeaf Publishing

India | USA | UK

Presentation by *BookLeaf Publishing*

Web: www.bookleafpub.com

E-mail: info@bookleafpub.com

ISBN: 9789358319880

First edition 2023

# DEDICATION

I dedicate this book, as I do my life, to my family.

# PREFACE

What's your specialist subject? It's you, isn't it?

Setting yourself the challenge to write a bunch of poems, the easy way out is to write about yourself. And I know all about taking the easy way out! It is easy to write about your life, your hopes, your dreams. The words come easy as the stories are already in your head.

In this collection, I look back at what made me into me. How my greatest defence mechanism, making people laugh, got me into trouble but also got me out of it again. There are highs and lows as I realise I might be one of the most cheerful pessimists in the world.

This book is also about so many of the wonderful people I have met along the way. Without them, this book has no meaning. Sadly, some of them are no longer with us, so I hope these ramblings are a way of keeping their spirits with us a bit longer.

These words are a love letter, an apology, a diary entry, a note of thanks and a how-not-to guide. I also hope that you find something of yourselves in this. Yes, even you!

However, my main hope is that you enjoy them. If not, I assume this book can be recycled or it'd make a great lining to your pet's cage.

# Being Born

On a Wednesday in August,
I was born.

I was a bit late.
Sorry about that, Mum.

I was a Leo,
born in the year of
the Monkey.
I still don't know
quite what
this means or
why it matters.

All I know is
a summer baby,
that's me.

# My Families

I love my family.
I always have,
and I always will.

However, I have a habit of
collecting families too.

I've got a few mums and dads,
and I call them that too.
I've got loads of brothers and sisters,
all part of the crew.

My friend's wife is French.
When they got married in France,
I was the only
English guest.

I don't speak French.
They didn't speak English.

However, I felt the warmth
and the love of the family.
I was included and
was treated like
I was just as

French as they were.

Language barriers mean nothing
when it comes to love and family.

Maybe that's why I love families so much.
I love mine the most,
obviously,
but I love the feel of family.
It is warm and inviting.
It is a light that never goes out.

To all my families,
wherever you may be.
To my mums, dads, brothers, and sisters.
I thank you and I love you all.

# New Start

When I was young,
Mum and Dad said we were going to have a
new house,
new school,
new friends.

I said no.
I didn't know why I couldn't stay at my
old house,
my old school,
with old friends.

We moved anyway.
When we moved, I didn't like our
new house,
new school,
with no friends.

It took a while but
eventually it became
our house,
my school,
with some friends.

I look back now,

and remember when it was a
new house,
new school,
new friends.

But it became part of me.
What was once new became
my house,
my school,
my friends.

# My Mate

One of my best friends is,
to be polite,
different.

I sometimes wonder if
his mouth kicks in
before his brain
does.

I remember one day,
at school,
he came over to me
rather angry and said:

"I can't believe it.
That witch of a
maths teacher
gave me a
detention!
Me!
Me?!
I didn't even do
anything!"

I looked confused.

"Well…" I said,
"You must have done
something…"

Then came the pause.

A very long pause.

I could hear the cogs
in his head grinding
as he worked it all out.

Then it came out:

"I mean, I threw a chair at her!"

I would like to say this
is the only example,
but it happened again
a year or so later.

We met up in the
Christmas holidays.
It was January and
just before we went
back to school,
when he said:

"So, we went out on
New Years and all these boys
started on me in the street
and I got involved in this
big punch up.
I didn't even do
anything!"

I looked confused.

"Well…" I said,
"You must have done
something…"

Then came the pause.

It was a longer pause
this time.

You could hear the engineers
spraying the cogs in his brain
with oil as they tried to get
them moving again.

Suddenly, it roared into life.

Then it came out:

"I mean, I did stand in the

middle of the road and shout
COME ON THEN!"

I'm going to be his
best man
one day.

This will be a much better
poem then some of the
sentimental rubbish you
usually hear at
weddings.

# Being Funny

I used to hate when someone
said I was funny.
It put me on the spot,
like I had to do it for money.

My humour will always
be my greatest defence.
I never have a go
or try to cause offence.

When I was at school,
I was the class clown.
I saw it as a service
to stop people feeling down.

We had emos and chavs
with me in between.
Quick wit was the way
I survived as a teen.

I tiptoed the line
between the jokes and the work.
I was walking on air
when I got a teacher to smirk.

A joke, some wit,
a silly voice, or impression.
Every path led me to
yet another digression.

We made our form tutor cry
with tears of laughter.
That cemented our place
as comedy kings thereafter.

Everyone at school
just wanted to laugh.
Every student, every year group,
every member of staff.

I had people ask me
to be funny on stage.
But I couldn't put it into words
or write it on a page.

I love making people laugh,
but it can't be a living.
There's not the same joy in a job
as there is in just giving.

I'm older now,
but I know I won't change.
I can still make a room laugh;
I've still got the range.

I'm still the class clown
but now I'm the teacher instead.
It's a trait of mine
that I will never put to bed.

It doesn't need to be laughter
that sweetens the mind.
So, if you can't be funny,
then perhaps just be kind.

I used to hate when someone
said I was funny.
But I've learnt to accept it:
I'm me and I'm funny.

# Those Four Lads

How can four lads
from Liverpool be,
such an influence
on someone like me.

By the time I was born,
one had already gone.
But that didn't matter,
as their music lived on.

From their rock and roll hits,
to tunes more mellow.
From their fools on hills,
to submarines of yellow.

Listening to their music,
made me pick up the guitar.
I ended up with a ukulele,
and still didn't get very far.

Their songs made you smile,
and you laughed at their jokes.
They were treated as messiahs,
but were just ordinary blokes.

They could do what they wanted,
with the world at their feet.
They even did an album cover,
where they just crossed the street.

I wish I could've been there,
to see them perform.
To see the fab four on stage,
to be in the eye of that storm.

My friends use to laugh at me,
dismissing their music as 'old'.
But I didn't really care,
because all I heard was gold.

So, thank you John,
and thank you Paul.
Thanks George and Ringo,
thank you for it all.

From that first hit single,
to the end of Let it Be.
Those four lads from Liverpool,
had a huge impact on me.

# Loving Your Team

It is impossible to love a human
like you love your team.

Your team can make the
worst week
even worse.

Your team can
let you down
regularly.

Your team can mess
with your emotions
in a way no
human can.

Your team will drain your heart,
mind,
and wallet
with no
apology.

And yet…

Your team can give you

the greatest moments
of your life.

Your team can provide
purpose and meaning
when you can't find it
anywhere else.

Your team can take you
on the ride of
your life.

Your team will make you
feel you
belong.

Maybe it's best that you can't love a human
like you love your team.

# The Last Time

If I knew it would be the last time I saw you,
I probably would have done things differently.

I would have recalled our happiest moments.
You would smile and nod as we reminisced.

I would have asked those questions
I never would have dared ask otherwise.
You would answer me honestly.

I would have made some mad suggestions
about what the future would look like.
You would laugh and call me crazy.

I would have thanked you for being you.
You would get embarrassed and never
accept the compliment.

I would then have given you the tightest hug I
could.
You would embrace the warmth and hold me
close
one last time.

Yes, if I knew it would be the last time I saw
you,
I certainly would have done things differently.

# That One Weekend

That one weekend
When we first got to meet.
That one weekend
You made me feel so complete.

That one weekend
I replay in my head.
That one weekend
I recall every word that you said.

That one weekend
When I poured my heart out.
That one weekend
With no fear and no doubt.

That one weekend
We sang our own duet.
That one weekend
How could I ever forget?

That one weekend
You took hold of my heart.
That one weekend
I wish I could restart.

That one weekend
I have stored in my mind.
That one weekend
Where I keep it confined.

That one weekend
Where I made you laugh.
That one weekend
Now just a photograph.

# Being A Student

Northampton Uni
and what it did for me
was set me up for my future.

I'd commute everyday
as I had no way to pay
the sky-high bills for a house.

I studied Drama
during the time of Obama
but in hindsight I'd have done something else.

You'd stand and perform
in dark rooms that weren't warm
and then somehow get a degree.

Luckily, I was bright
I'd write an essay in a night
and submit it with minutes to spare.

I lived without fear
knowing what they wanted to hear
which meant I was lazy and slack.

There was never confusion

but there was disillusion
as I waited for it all to be over.

The one thing I treasure
from those years of no pleasure
are the friends who I still love today.

When I look back at Uni
I find I didn't like me
maybe that's why I didn't enjoy it.

# Getting Love Wrong

I got love wrong and I'm sorry.

I thought I knew love and could control it.

I thought that love would lead to something.

I used love to get what I wanted.

I would mistake other things for love.

I took advantage of what love could offer.

I took love for granted.

I never truly understood love.

I owe love an apology.

I don't think love will ever forgive me.

I'm sorry love.

# The Addict's Lament

24

I'll have one more today and then that's it.
I could give up tomorrow and not miss it one bit.

I suppose I will stop at the start of next week.
Maybe one more and then I'll reach the peak.

I don't need this; I just enjoy it for fun.
I like to have lots, but I'd be happy with one.

I just feel happier when I have one in my
possession.
Just because I enjoy it regularly doesn't make it
an obsession.

It doesn't influence everything that I do.
I can still enjoy some other things too.

If I can't enjoy it then what will be will be.
The world will keep spinning and I'll still be me.

I can go without; I don't need it for the day.
But what about tomorrow? Will I be ok?

# Being Inspired

I told my mum
I wanted to be a teacher.
I told her this to
shut her up at
parents evening when
I was 16.

It worked.

Mum is also a teacher, you see,
so she got me some
work experience
at her school.

A special school, it is,
for those with
special needs.

Here I met one of the biggest
influences on my career.

I worked with
one of the kindest people
I have ever met.
He taught the

youngest pupils.
The only primary age
pupils in
the school.

He spoke softly
and everyone listened.
His words were
calming
and soothed the class,
like a piece of
classical music.

He had those
six pupils
in the palm of
his hand.

I was inspired and
I tried so hard to
be like him when
I started training to
be a teacher.

It never worked.

Thankfully,
I got a job
alongside him after

I qualified.
He was my mentor
and saw me through
those tough
first few years.

Whatever I do in the future,
I will be forever
indebted to
the man who helped me
get that job.

The job I suggested
to my mum
all those years before.

Nice one, Simon,
I will be forever grateful.

# Teaching Acronyms

Post
Graduate
Certificate of
Education

Disclosure and
Barring
Service

Newly
Qualified
Teacher

Planning
Preparation and
Assessment time

Continual
Professional
Development

Special
Educational
Needs

Attention
Deficit
Hyperactivity
Disorder

Autism
Spectrum
Disorder

Save
Our
Sanity

# Thank You

Thank you for being there
and looking out for me.
Your impact goes further
than your eyes can see.

Thank you for listening
and helping me out.
It's nicer to chat than
to rant or shout.

Thank you for your support
with my mental health.
You provide the breath to
life itself.

Thank you for the smile
that brightens your face.
You make the darkest times
into the happiest place.

Thank you for the support
through thick and thin.
My glass is half empty,
but I feel like I can win.

Thank you for the hugs
and holding me tight.
It keeps away the demons
that pester me at night.

Thank you for showing me
another way to be.
For teaching me how
to be a better me.

Thank you for loving me
for who I am.
Every day I try to repay you
in any way I can.

# What Kids Say

I thought teaching was easy until a kid spoke to me.
He asked me how to spell GCSE.

I found teaching okay until this one time.
A kid asked if Ed Sheeran wrote a nursery rhyme.

I thought I was great and found teaching a whizz.
A kid then stopped assembly to ask when Christmas is.

I thought teaching was all about the potential you unlock.
Until a kid asked in Sex-Ed if it was safe to use a sock.

I thought I had everything in teaching planned.
Then a kid described the Beatles as 'another boy band'.

I thought I had this teaching lark sussed.
I showed a class my favourite comedy and nobody was fussed.

Maybe I've still got a lot of teaching to learn.
I wonder how much a book of kid's quotes
would earn?

# Fading Away

There is nothing worse than watching someone
you love fade away.
A character full of colour becomes a shadow full
of grey.

You try looking for answers in reports and in
books.
And your life fills with people and their
sympathetic looks.

You find yourself grateful for things long taken
for granted.
Your hope goes to war with the pessimism that's
implanted.

We're not scared to die but we're scared to be
dying.
You smile on the outside when inside you're
crying.

However long we have, we will always want
more.
Anything to put off what the future has in store.

Every time you see them, you can't find the
words to say.
You have no spells or magic words to make
everything okay.

Just make sure they know that you will always
be there.
You know they'd do the same, so it seems only
fair.

Remember the colour that came before the grey.
Because in your head and your heart they can
never fade away.

# How to Help

We all would help the homeless,
if they just took card.
That way, we could help them all,
it wouldn't be so hard.

They all have my sympathy,
and I don't mean to be funny.
But it's the 21st century now,
and I don't carry real money.

We all make our excuses,
and say we have to dash.
It's not that we don't want to help,
it's that we don't have the cash.

If we gave the homeless a special card,
they could buy the things they need.
That'd encourage the cynical few,
who say they spend it all on weed.

A card could help someone start their new life,
get off the streets and then get clean.
They don't need cash or sympathy,
all they need is a card machine.

It can't be easy for the homeless,
every day can seem pretty crap.
So what if we all could help them,
with a smile and a tap.

Nobody deserves to be homeless,
we'd all want that second chance.
So if they could take contactless,
I'd give them more than a glance.

# Holding

When my friend was killed,
I was just 17.

I walked in the door from work,
and you said nothing.

My eyes filled with tears as
you looked at me.

It was then that the
events of the day
hit me like a train.

You just put out your arms and
held me, as I sobbed on your shoulder
like a child.

When you got ill,
I was no longer 17.

I walked in the door from work,
and you said nothing.

Your eyes filled with tears as
you looked at me.

It was then the
effects of your treatment
hit you like a train.

I just put out my arms and
held you, as you sobbed on my shoulder
like a child.

You held me and I held you.

# Season's Eatings

Football and food go hand in hand.
My two greatest loves, I'll try to make you
understand.

Following your team away can drive anyone
crackers.
But it can be remedied with just a few words:
"Anyone fancy a Maccas?"

You've travelled 200 miles and you're 3-0
down.
But a decent pie and Bovril can turn your day
upside down.

The only highlight on the pitch was an on target
free kick.
Cheer up, get some grub, enough to make you
feel sick.

A dead rubber in April with your season down
the pan.
The bitter tastes sweeter if there's some good
footy scran.

A pie or a burger or a pasty or some chips.

Your team lives in your heart, the food lives on your hips.

Going up and down the country hoping your team finds some form.
Your only solace is a snack that is tasty and warm.

So, at times when your team gets you doubting yourself.
It's the snacks in the stands that protect your mental health.

Yes, football and food go hand in hand.
I don't expect you to agree, I just hope you understand.

# The End

21

Well, I guess that's it,
I hope you've had fun.
We're at the last poem,
we're at poem 21.

So, what have we learnt?
Probably not much.
Just a few pointless stories
about such and such.